The Narcissist and Me

The Relationship That Should Not Have Been

By: Nikki J. Moore

D1244894

Dedicated to all the men and women who are or have been in a toxic narcissistic relationship.

Help us O Lord to recognize the signs and the red flags.

1

This is a true story about a relationship that should not have been.

Why? Because I found myself in a relationship with a narcissist.

There are specific characteristics attributed to narcissistic peoples. Narcissists are known to have excessive admiration for themselves. They harbor a deep demand for constant attention and adoration. They think they are the center of the universe and the world revolves or should revolve around *them*. They are vain, selfish, and have inflated egos that give them a great sense of self-importance while disregarding others' feelings, wants, and needs. And they're apathetic and envious of others; or they cling to the belief that everybody else is envious of *them*.

I share this particular story to help those that also find themselves in a relationship with someone that's considered to be a narcissist or exhibit narcissistic behaviors.

I didn't listen to God when I should have and I was convinced that my ex-boyfriend was a blessing from Him when he was inarguably the complete opposite. I was totally wrong and impatient and made the wrong choices thinking that this man was the man that God meant for me to be with.

In wanting love so badly, I made quite a few wrong choices and took many wrong turns.

This is my journey, my struggle. A journey that put me in a scenario that was nightmarish and almost defeating. A journey that taught me an extremely invaluable lesson.

Briefly mentioned in my second book, *The Journey Continues for Your Glory*, here is the whole story. And the whole truth. One that will hopefully teach those out there a lesson in patience and awareness. That not every seemingly and initially perfect romantic situation paints an impeccable and pretty picture for the future of that relationship. That what started off as the makings of a fairytale romance ended up being a tale of abuse, misery, and deception.

I cannot recall how I found my ex-boyfriend Shamari's profile on Facebook, but when I saw it and glanced through several of his pictures, I thought he was a gorgeous man. I briefly scanned his profile and really liked what I saw. I thought, throwing caution to the wind, that I'd say hello to him, not really expecting a response back. Or having any expectations at all.

Quite a bit of time went by after my difficult divorce and I thought I'd try and gradually get back into the dating scene again. I didn't get my hopes too high and I only wanted to take things slowly. I wasn't ready to remarry or in a hurry to get into another committed relationship, but I wanted to date and just get to know people; perhaps at the very least make new friends.

A month had gone by and one day I received a notification on my phone. It was Shamari. He was finally saying hello back. I was curious and did ask why he waited a month.

"I had to make sure you weren't catfishing me or anything like that," Shamari said.

Very good point! I heard that! I just laughed when he told me that though.

3

Shamari seemed laidback and like a very easy person to talk to. We connected instantaneously and had so much in common; speaking to one another as if we had known each other for years. We really hit it off and I really liked him because he was just such a charming and fun-loving guy. He was also very interesting, articulate, and seemed down-to-earth.

One thing that really drew me to him was his knowledge of the Word and his faith in God. And we spent hours talking about God and ministry. To me, it felt like heaven. Finally, someone I could talk to about the Lord and scripture!

I loved listening to Shamari talk about the gospel. This man was truly on fire for the Lord, I thought. I was just amazed at what I was hearing. The things he'd say and how passionately he expressed it.

We would do bible study one-on-one before we discussed other topics. And I would tell myself, "God! This has got to be the man you are sending me!"

He was everything I was asking Him for in a man.

We called each other every day. I couldn't believe someone this young and fine could show this much interest in me, an older woman. Shamari was 46, good-looking, smart, and seemed to have such a good head on his shoulders.

There's no way to put into words just how happy I was. Coworkers and friends noticed this.

"Okay! Who is he?" asked one of my coworkers. "Because whoever he is has you beaming! He's brought such a glow to you, Nikki."

"He's just a friend. Someone that I am getting to know because I'm not sure if it'll even last since he's younger," I said. I then added casually, "He may find some younger lady or a lady his age to start talking to, you never know."

At that point in my life and shortly after my divorce, I didn't want to get my hopes up only to be let down badly in the end. I was convinced it was only the age difference that would be the problem; not his personality, since I had very little doubt about the kind of person he was, for he seemed so perfect at the time. I also thought he was just looking for friends; just someone to talk to and nothing more.

We FaceTimed and texted often. He would always promptly answer every single text and call. Shamari was such a sweetheart and I felt right back in high school; anxious and excited to get home so I could get on the phone with the hot guy in my class I was crushing on. He was dependable. He was reliable. And he always responded right away. Even when he was busy at work, he'd let me know anyway that he was working but that he'd get back to me once he had a moment free. And he always did.

Shamari would send cute little videos of him lip-syncing to songs he knew I'd like. Songs with deep meaning as if communicating the songs' messages to tell me that's how he felt about me.

He had sent these videos of the songs he was pretending to serenade me with and I loved every one of them. I enjoyed them so much that I asked if he could send one every day if he could. And he did, always picking a song that had a profound message.

I couldn't believe that I found someone like Shamari. Someone that made me feel like a new woman. Someone that helped put all the pieces back together after a divorce I was certain at one point I wouldn't be able to recover from.

He made me feel confident. And I was confident my heart would mend and that when it came to romantic

2

"Every word in this song; that is how I feel about you and I mean that," Shamari said.

"Are you sure about that?" I responded with a smile, wanting to be reassured even though I was certain he meant it.

"Yes. Absolutely," he replied very cordially.

One evening we were chatting via FaceTime; he was lying in bed and he began to cry.

"What's wrong," I asked, with deep concern. "I didn't say anything that hurt your feelings, did I?"

"No," Shamari said. "It isn't that at all."

"What then?"

"It's just...," he took a pause. He then added with heartbreaking sincerity, "I'm crying because...I can't believe that God would send me a wonderful woman like you."

"That is so sweet," I said with a smile and I'm pretty sure I blushed.

I then knew at that very moment Shamari's feelings for me were genuine and not only genuine, but getting stronger every day.

Another few months passed before he told me, "I love you."

His declaration rather blindsided me—in a good way of course. It had been a long time since a man had told me he loved me. And a part of me was certain I'd never hear that again.

Shamari would text a little prayer on my phone each morning. A sweet prayer that reaffirmed his faith in God and his willingness to take that spiritual journey with me.

"This has got to be the man you are sending to me," I'd pray, feeling very sure and like I was on top of the world.

Shamari had unquestionably won me over. He was winning every bit of my heart with all the things he did. All the things he said. And no longer did I harp on his age or how beautiful he was on the outside because he was so much more inside. I feared I was going to wake up and discover it was all a dream. I just couldn't believe that it was me he wanted. Of all the women I'm sure he could have had; I was his choice and his choice only. And because of him I regained my self-confidence in its entirety. I think it really was *only* the age difference that made me hesitant, but I was sure about everything else with him.

I asked Shamari again if the age difference was eventually going to be problematic. He assured that it wouldn't.

"It doesn't matter," he said. "Because it's all about your beautiful heart and soul. You are a very pretty woman inside and out." And he reminded me always how attracted he was to me.

Tears of joy ran down my face. I couldn't believe what I was hearing but I loved it. And at that time, I don't think I could have thanked God enough. He told me he loved me every day and a couple more months had passed, I started to feel the same way about him.

At this point, we still hadn't met in person. But I knew that day would come very soon and I couldn't wait. I knew it was right and I knew it just had to be him.

After almost a year, we talked about so much. Our conversations were deep and we never ran out of things to say in the hours we'd spend on FaceTime or on calls.

Shamari too had children and he talked about how they were the world to him, which made me fall even harder for him.

With all the time that had passed, it was beginning to torture me that I couldn't kiss him or wrap my arms around him. I wanted those things to happen so badly at that point, I just had to find a way to make it so.

I wanted to hear everything that he had to say face-to-face. I wanted to feel the touch of Shamari's hand. I needed to hear him say that he loved me in person.

Shamari had also a very charitable spirit. He started his own business and worked with people with drug and alcohol addiction and worked diligently towards helping them rehabilitate.

"It brings me joy knowing that I give back to others," Shamari said to me. "It's in my heart to help those who are unable to help themselves." His earnestness. The way he said it. He was one of the most selfless people I had ever met.

One day, Shamari FaceTimed me when he was at work to show me the kinds of people he worked with. He introduced me to them via the video chat and I was able to say hello to all of them. The expression on his face was indescribable. I could tell he was passionate about what he did and that he was excited to make me a part of his world.

It was a breath of fresh air knowing that I met someone as enthusiastic about helping others as I was. I love being generous and being a blessing to other people. I loved every moment I got to know him. I shared with Shamari how I ran my own nonprofit for five years giving support to families in need; but that I had trouble maintaining the business because of all that I had gone through (in regards to my divorce and being a survivor of sexual abuse as a child and the emotional toll it had taken in my life; though I didn't go into those details with him).

Shamari was very supportive and encouraging. He tried to convince me to start it back up because so many people needed help out there and that I was too strong a woman to let past adversities prevent me from accomplishing my goals. He emphasized that this was God's calling for me and that by continuing to give back to the community, it would really aid in the healing process overall. I told him it was something that I had to give hard thought to. Shamari told me to pray about it because he believed in his heart it was something God would want me to start back up again.

This was also when I realized Shamari would be there to lift me up. To always tell me to be a go-getter when I wasn't feeling like one. That I would succeed and that I could do it. And considering all I had been through; his inspiration was the very thing I needed. I couldn't allow my past define and impact my present and my future in a negative way. It would prove detrimental and my past problems couldn't continue to be that anvil tied to my waist weighing me down. I had to push past all that and Shamari was there to help me.

3

Shamari was so fine! I was loving him! I loved everything about him! His style. His looks. His personality. His faith. And his swagger and how he treated me with utmost respect. Shamari was chivalrous. Giving me that old school kind of love. He was winning every part of me the more I got to know him. He sent handsome pictures of himself along with more cute lip-syncing videos. He was a "love-bomb!" Bursting with endless affirmations of love; endless compliments about how beautiful I was; constant entertaining fantasies of getting away together to far-off places; and so on!

He was photogenic and he looked so good in all his pictures, I began thinking about him in ways I knew I shouldn't have. I felt guilty for wanting sexually a man I hadn't yet met face-to-face, but I couldn't help it.

I wanted to kiss him. Touch him. And hold him. And it only got stronger the more we were communicating and the more we shared our feelings towards one another. I was very physically-attracted to him and he admitted his feelings were mutual.

Shamari lived just outside New York City, but I was willing to travel the 200 miles for just one touch; one kiss. I just wanted to be with him so much it hurt!

We had regularly deliberated over me coming to visit but we never had a set plan and couldn't agree solidly on one whenever it was brought up. But the more time that had passed, the more anxious I became.

Finally, when it was brought up again, this time we came to an agreement. We figured out a time that fit both our schedules. Being a gentleman, Shamari said it was all right for me to stay at his place and that I could sleep in his room while he took the sofa in the living room. This made me feel more certain about him.

I could barely catch my breath as I realized our meeting was about to become a reality. I booked my flight and made all the travel arrangements. I told him everything was a go and Shamari expressed how excited he was that he was finally going to meet me.

It was about a month before the trip and I reached out to him one day. It was the first time in the almost one-year that we have been communicating in which I did not receive an immediate response from him. It was uncharacteristic, but all things considered, I figured he got really tied up at work or perhaps there was some kind of family emergency that he'd make me aware of later that day.

Well…that evening, I sent another text but again, nothing. The very next morning, I woke up hoping that I'd see a text or maybe a Facebook message had popped up while I was sleeping, but still, no response despite them having read receipts.

Those two days turned to a week and then another. It completely baffled as well as worried me because this wasn't like him at all.

Did he ghost me, I thought?

Then, I dreaded the possibility that perhaps there either was already another woman, or that he JUST met one. It also crossed my mind that he was still married and didn't tell me.

I was so confused, so frustrated, and ultimately heartbroken that I sent one more text after three weeks or so to tell Shamari I was canceling my trip. At the very least, maybe he got cold feet and didn't want me to come up after all, I thought. But why couldn't he have just said that? I would have understood. It can be a little scary asking a woman you've never seen in person to come stay with you for several days, especially since all your communication was through social media, phone calls, FaceTime, and texts.

I just couldn't comprehend the reasoning behind his invitation only to ghost me once the travel arrangements had been made and everything was set in stone and my time off work had been approved. It also wasn't like I was pressuring him or rushing things. If he wasn't ready to see me, that is all he had to say. Ghosting someone is the most cowardly thing a person can do, I thought; and considering the effort I put forth in making the plans, it was also a waste (and kind of cruel if it was intentional, which I later realized it was).

Several days before the trip, I was able to cancel the reservations without penalty. Once I did, I texted Shamari and let him know I made the cancellations and I wouldn't be coming up.

Then, the next day is when I heard back from him. Perfect timing! What supposedly had happened was that his business had run into, to the best of my knowledge and recollection, legal or financial trouble or both; and these problems were mounting one after the other and quickly snowballing, which caused a great deal of stress amongst he and his coworkers.

Shamari was supposedly dealing with insurmountable anxiety that basically caused him to shut down, which he claimed was the reasoning for his silence. I am sympathetic to people being stricken with work-related stress; stress so bad that it can cause us to shut down sometimes. But not to sound selfish, how long would it have taken him and how difficult would it have been to just send *one text* saying, "I'm sorry. Dealing with a work crisis. Will fill you in soon"? OR "Will fill you in when you come up to visit. Look forward to seeing you." Something!

The problem was, I believed him. Not because I genuinely did, but because I wanted to believe him. I was forgiving, and then told him that whenever he was really truly ready for me to come visit to please notify me. Shamari apologized once again and told me he would. After the high and anticipation I felt in the past several months and the weeks leading up to the trip, I felt jilted, lost, and just hung my head down. I wouldn't feel his arms wrapped around me and his lips on mine once he greeted me at the airport, seeing him in-person for the very first time.

Another few months passed and now he was talking about coming down to visit me instead. He was

18

still in New York, but had relocated just west of Albany for reasons he wouldn't disclose.

Shamari then made me aware of all these problems he was having at his new place. His roommate was supposedly a younger woman with children. And her children were stealing from him.

"Why are you still there?" I asked, a bit cautiously as I wasn't really sure what to believe, especially now with this younger female roommate in his life.

"I have nowhere else to go," said Shamari. "I'm pretty much stuck here right now and I'm so stressed out because of her kids and the fact that she's so selfish."

Our engaging and romantic conversations from before turned into venting sessions in which he continuously griped about how unhappy he was at his new place and how angry he was about his roommate's children stealing from him all the time. It was a stark contrast and completely deterring because Shamari became so negative and so depressing. But I felt very sorry for him and offered to let him come visit me for a few weeks so he could escape and de-stress for a while.

"You really mean that?" Shamari asked.

19

"Yes," I replied. "But I live in a one-bedroom apartment so you'll have to sleep on the couch if that's okay."

"That is totally fine," Shamari said, with an immense sigh of relief.

After that, I felt I got shades of the old Shamari back. He sounded like the man I got to know again, which, to be perfectly honest, made me excited all over again and made me feel much better about his upcoming visit.

4

The old Shamari returned, I thought. We were back to texting, conversing via FaceTime, and talking on the phone almost every day as he was the Shamari that knocked me off my feet; showered me with praise and love; and talked about the things that made me look forward to our conversations. He didn't let me down at all this time.

He also sent a screenshot of the train ticket to prove he was coming down to visit, which included the dates and times, which was sometime in mid-June.

My excitement grew once again and I was feeling much better, more relaxed, and certain this time. I even started counting down the days until his arrival.

The days we talked leading up to his trip, I asked what he would like to eat and things he would like to do. He wasn't picky at all and told me he didn't care as long as he was with me.

One day before his departure from New York, the memory of his ghosting me hit me suddenly like a bullet train. I was also dreading that once he saw me in-person he was going to be disappointed or that he wouldn't like me and that I wasn't the woman he wanted to be with after all.

So, that morning we were texting each other as he was on the train and he and I were very uneasy and almost terrified about the whole thing. He told me he too felt I was going to take one look at him and think he wasn't as attractive in person or that we were suddenly going to realize the chemistry wasn't there after all. Shamari also feared he wasn't going to have what I was looking for in a man.

"It'll be okay Shamari, I promise," I assured him. "Just get here safely and we'll take it one day at a time."

"Thank you, wifey," Shamari said. And when I heard him call me *wifey*, my doubts were erased. I was so happy because he was truly the Shamari again I had been talking to right before I was supposed to travel up to see him.

He wouldn't arrive in Virginia until 2:30pm, but we talked and texted back and forth the whole way through.

On my drive to the train station in Alexandria, I felt really sick to my stomach. The butterflies were fluttering wildly within.

I pulled into the train station near the King St. metro and parked. I texted Shamari to get an idea of his current location and ETA, asking him what he saw out his window, etcetera.

He told me he was passing the Jefferson Memorial.

"Oh, my goodness!" I exclaimed; a bit on edge. "You are very close!"

"Oh Nikki!" he said, sounding just as nervous. "I really hope that I am all that you are looking for and that I look okay."

I let him know the feeling was mutual.

I was talking to my girlfriend on the phone and it seemed like everyone was very curious about Shamari. Most importantly, my close friends seemed happy for me and hoped that I would be just as happy with him in person as I was when talking and getting to know him via text and call.

She remained on the phone with me and I told her I was very excited but also felt like throwing up. She just laughed hysterically.

Then, his train pulled into the station.

"Debbie, here comes the train, I'm so nervous I'm going to pee!" I said, then followed it with a brief bout of nervous laughter.

"Girl, you will be fine," she said.

Debbie remained on the phone with me until Shamari came into view.

"I see him, there he is!" I told her as he exited the train unto the platform. "I got to go now."

"Everything will be okay," she replied. "You got this Nikki."

I was standing at the driver's side when his eyes met mine. I waved eagerly; my arms raised high into the air. He approached me holding a huge, angelic grin on his face until we were within a few feet of one another.

"Aren't you gonna come give me a hug?" he asked as he set his bag down next to the passenger's side of my car.

I went around and gave him a hug. He kissed me on the lips, which was unexpected, but I welcomed it nonetheless.

"Are you still nervous now?" I asked.

"No," replied Shamari. "Now that I have seen you. You?"

"Just a little," I told him. "But not as bad as before."

We got in the car and headed back in the direction of my apartment. We stopped at a few places and ran a couple of errands he needed to quickly run before we got back home. We had great conversation during the drive just like we had over the phone leading up to this meeting. He told me he'd never been to Virginia before and that the parks and trees seemed beautiful.

We returned to my place and when we got inside, I told him to make himself at home. He asked if I had any strict rules as far as the dos and don'ts of my apartment were concerned. I just told him I didn't like the lights on all the time, especially in rooms that weren't being used. To clean up after himself when he was finished cooking or eating. And to just keep the bathroom neat. Other than that, I was good.

I was in the kitchen washing the dishes after dinner when Shamari said, "Nikki. Please don't get mad or uncomfortable or take this the wrong way. I say this as a compliment, not to be out of order. But you are looking *good* in those jeans!"

I roared with laughter but I was completely
flattered. I know I must've blushed.

"Thank you," I said with a great big smile.

He then asked me to come join him on the couch.
I got comfortable next to him and we talked for several
minutes. Then, he reached over and pulled me to him and
started kissing me gently. We moved in closer to one
another as we began to kiss more passionately. I got to
admit, it felt great to be kissed, though in the back of my
mind I knew it was wrong because even though we had
been talking for almost a year, we had just met face-to-
face that day and it was probably too fast. But the touch of
his lips and the feeling of his skin, I was loving it!

It was something I had been longing for. To kiss
him and feel his arms wrapped tightly around me. I knew
being in close quarters, let alone letting him stay at my
place probably wasn't the wisest, but I was craving his
touch and some companionship that I didn't even care
what was appropriate and what was not, anymore.

5

Three days in and I did not question at all our compatibility. We had so much fun together. We played tennis almost every day and I would accompany him to the pool. I loved lying poolside while I watched him swim (I don't do pools myself, LOL). We also watched *Family Feud* and played along to see how many answers we could get before they were revealed to the contestants.

He shared fond and hilarious memories of his childhood and we entertained the idea of doing ministry together. I really honestly felt there was nothing significant that could go wrong because we got along so well and I enjoyed having him with me. Yes, the physical aspect of the relationship was great, but I loved more just spending time with him and talking. That part felt so much more meaningful and we just had so much else in common.

We engaged in deep conversations when we'd go out to dinner, never running out of things to say. He had won my heart and I felt safer and safer with him, next making a decision I'd come to eventually regret. The fourth night of his stay, we had sex.

I knew deep down it was something I probably shouldn't have even jumped into despite us talking for almost a year. He too told me he felt a bit guilty for doing it, but our desires were inescapable and irrepressible, it was something we could no longer hold back.

The next morning, we awoke and decided to say a prayer together. A prayer for forgiveness for engaging in something we knew God didn't want for us just yet (or ever). For the remainder of the trip, he vowed to remain on the couch and we took an oath of chastity as we felt the sexual aspect wasn't as important at that time. I thought it was very civil of him, though the experience did cast some doubt that perhaps what we did was a one-and-done deal and he'd quickly lose interest since there was no longer that mystery in the relationship.

At that moment, I felt I needed to be reassured once more.

"Why me?" I asked. "Of all the women in the world."

"Why not you, Nikki," replied Shamari. We smiled at one another and then just made our way to the community pool.

It was the second week of his stay and we were going to the Fourth of July Parade. Despite the day being humid and probably the hottest it's been in years, the time spent together certainly made up for it...until after the parade when we had our first argument.

I cannot quite recall what the argument was exactly about but I do remember it being over something infinitesimal that somehow escalated, thanks in large part to him. This was the beginning of a darker chapter of a relationship that was seemingly perfect...until it wasn't. He was a man I thought was well-mannered and wanted much of the same things out of life I did, until he wasn't. A monster that would reveal the ugliest parts of him thinking he could manipulate me and gain control hoping I'd surrender all that I was to open the door for his emotional and psychological abuse.

We didn't speak to each other for the remainder of the evening as I was in my room, door closed, on edge while watching television while he was in the living room doing the same, expecting me to cave and apologize and admit fault for something *he* turned into a big deal, not me.

Then, he got up, opened my door, and stood at the threshold with an expression on his face that was almost terrifying.

Shamari then said, "Nikki! Be careful! Because you don't know who you are talking to and who you're dealing with!"

Then, he shut the door and that was it and I almost knew straightaway I was probably dealing with someone that was not who I thought. I almost felt the Holy Spirit trying to convey a message; a strong message. Warning me this person had a dark side that was going to challenge me and my faith. I almost felt God move through me as I was laying there, hearing those words Shamari so eerily and chillingly spoke. But because I was so deep into my feelings for Shamari, I didn't want to believe this was a warning. I chose to ignore the Holy Spirit.

Instead, I would fall deep into an obsession that would cause me to completely disregard what my head, my heart, and the higher powers were trying to tell me. This man was bad news, but I wanted very much to believe his good would outweigh that bad and that we were truly in love.

Once upon a time, I mentioned briefly in my second book, *The Journey Continues for Your Glory*, that by the third week of one of Shamari's stays I had to actually call the police on him. He was diagnosed with bipolar disorder and he couldn't manage his bouts of rage. But also, there was something much deeper. And I was sailing my ship right into the eye of the hurricane.

On top of being verbally abusive when he couldn't get his anger under control, he would do things that were flat-out mentally-cruel. One day during that first visit, when we had another tiff about his bad habits, he deliberately left every light on and secretly turned my security camera so that the apartment was out of view, which I found very disturbing.

Then, he showed a more extreme side and I had to ask him to leave the house, not caring where he went as long as it was away from me. He then begged to stay at least until he received the money that he said was being sent to him so that he could find a new place to go.

It was a Friday when it was officially time for him to leave and everything felt different that day. Me and Shamari were back to "normal." From noon that day until eight that evening, we talked and talked and our

31

conversations were just like before. His train was due to leave the station in Old Town Manassas at around 8:30.

But for those eight hours, we never turned on the TV for distraction or engaged in other little diversions to simply pass the time. It was back to the fun and engaging conversations of before and *now* I no longer wanted him to leave.

Maybe his moods were brought about by his current living situation. Maybe he wasn't really that bad of a guy after all and he was just going through a difficult time.

It was time to go to the station and I felt a deep sadness. I genuinely didn't want for him to leave. At the end of his stay, I got the old Shamari back and I thought he was better. I wanted to believe this side of him was his true self, his better self; the man that I fell in love with and was convinced loved me back. He got on the train and waved from the window and I couldn't help myself, tears streamed down my face. I was really going to miss him.

I cried the whole drive home. I got back to the apartment and all I saw was us. Shamari and me. Where we lay. Where we kissed. All the things we did. Where we sat and ate. Where we watched TV. Everything.

Man! I felt so incredibly heartbroken that I just laid in bed and cried like a baby. But in believing that he was his so-called self again, it didn't take long before those authentic feelings of love quickly faded into ones I'd have difficulty putting into words.

6

I reached out to him not too long after that and suddenly Shamari was angry. He, for some strange reason, was angry with *me*.

He informed me that he would have to move to New Jersey to live in a homeless shelter and actually (and very inexplicably) blamed *me* for that. I had no idea why, but I guess his trip down to Virginia had something to do with it, I don't know. The way he said it was pure incoherent nonsense honestly. But I think he was scapegoating me as a way to avoid taking responsibility for his own actions, whatever they were and whatever happened. Another part of me believed another woman was probably involved. I could feel it inside and I didn't like the feeling one bit.

Yet just to be nice, I still would call and check in on him until he reached New Jersey but his blame-gaming persisted. Shamari argued that I didn't care that he was starving on the streets. That I didn't care he would have to live in a shelter if they were even able to take him that day.

I felt guilty. Not because I believed that any of that was my fault, but because I just couldn't bear the thought of him wandering the streets with nowhere to go and no one to turn to. And so, get ready for this, I sent him money.

I sent him money for food and actually felt so sorry for him that I even asked him to come back to Virginia.

"Please, just come back to me," I said with aching in my voice. "I miss you so much and I want you here with me. I know you're going through a very difficult time and I love you. I'm in love with you and I know when you were here there was something."

He professed his love back and was calm and collected again. Shamari then told me that he would love for nothing more than to return to me and told me he would if he could, but that he was broke, completely penniless and couldn't afford to make the trip down.

And so, yes, you guessed it, I sent him more money.

After he received it, he called me the next day to tell me he was taking the bus down and that he was at the station waiting for departure. I was so happy because he would be on his way back to me that night.

He'd be on a bus from Albany to Woodbridge, Virginia. The trip would take approximately 12 hours, departing at 2:30 pm and arriving in Virginia a little after 2:00 am.

"Please don't fall asleep on me and leave me hanging," Shamari said jokingly.

"I would never do that Shamari," I said with a chuckle. "I will definitely be up because I am so excited that you are coming back. It'll be hard to sleep anyway."

I was indeed excited, but unlike the last trip, I didn't check up on him or call or ask about his current location every hour or so. We texted like crazy when he first came down to Virginia, but while filled with overwhelming excitement then, I kept my cool as best I could this time around.

Night came and I was starting to count down the hours. Right before 10 or so, I actually nodded off. When I woke up it was around 1:30 am. The anticipation hit and my adrenaline was high, so I was wide awake and energetic, getting ready as quickly as I could to go to the bus station.

After washing my face and brushing my teeth, I felt those same butterflies aflutter as I stepped out the

36

door. I couldn't understand why I was feeling this way, but I was just as nervous as if meeting him for the first time.

I got to the bus station at around 2:25 and I was a little surprised to see that the station was almost completely deserted. I was one of only two cars in the parking lot. I waited in my car and locked the doors now feeling a little nervous about being the only one at the dark station lot with the exception of what was probably an employee's vehicle.

It was now 2:45. I told myself I'd give it five more minutes and if the bus didn't arrive, I'd call the station agent.

Those five minutes passed and I finally decided to call in and get an estimated time of arrival on the bus or see if they can track its current location. The young man I spoke with told me that there was *a* bus that was running late but would be arriving soon. I felt a bit relieved so I continued waiting patiently.

3:15 and I decided to call once again. This time a young lady picked up.

"Good evening miss," I said. "I'm just calling to see what time the bus that departed Albany, New York is estimated to arrive."

She went silent and took a rather long, almost uncomfortable pause.

"Ma'am," she said. "I'm sorry, but we have no buses coming from Albany, New York."

"Wait…what do you mean?" I asked with a stutter and in complete disbelief. "You're kidding, right?"

"No ma'am, I'm not, sorry. We don't have any or had any buses arriving from New York today."

"Any possible chance it was a transfer maybe?" I was desperate, doing everything I could to quell my anguish and feelings of denial. "Maybe the bus came from Albany but passengers had to transfer at a midway point?"

"Sorry miss," she said very apologetically. "The bus that's arriving is a northbound bus from Charlotte, North Carolina."

My heart honestly felt it could have just exploded out of my chest. I was extremely confused and devastated. Not to mention, I felt like a complete idiot. This man took my money and didn't even come here.

I cried all the way home. I climbed back in bed and just cried myself to sleep. It killed me that I could do something out of the kindness of my heart and be completely betrayed and used this way. Boy! Was I destroyed by this!

38

I attempted to call him later that morning but he didn't answer; I think he refused to answer. I left him a voicemail and texted him; and I absolutely told him off. And then I did my best to press on and regather. I moved on with the mindset that I was no longer going to see or hear from him again. And I didn't want to after what he did to me.

It wasn't easy to pick myself back up, but I couldn't let his deceit and abandonment redefine me negatively either. I wasn't going to be that sulking, hapless woman that lets something like this shatter her and paralyze her for months on end. I would move on and I would move on knowing that I was much better off without him.

Everything had finally gotten back on track for me and I felt I was back in a place that was healthy for me emotionally and mentally.

But, after almost a year had gone by, Shamari texts me.

7

When comparing the good vs. bad, and getting to know him for a little over a year, it was becoming apparent how manipulative he was and that he'd say just about anything to get what he wanted from me. I knew I was dancing with the devil trying to pursue anything with someone as conniving and selfish as he was, but I chose to overlook his flaws. I was just drawn too much to his good looks, outward appearance, and what he initially led me to believe he was that I decided to ignore the truth; the truth being that he was a predatory person preying on women like me.

Shamari was now in Jersey City and I went up to New York City not long after he reached out to me again after standing me up when I sent him money to come down to Virginia. I know it was foolish, but I did let him know that I happened to be in New York if he wanted to meet up and chat for a bit; explain himself.

Yes, it was a crazy thing to do. I shouldn't have even bothered with him, but I wasn't really so much trying to mold him into the man I thought I fell in love with so much as I was just trying to understand him and perhaps get some closure.

We made plans to meet up. I did want to see him and just wanted to talk to him again hoping that shades of the old Shamari would somehow resurface. It was insane to even think anything could possibly be salvaged, especially when his excuse for not coming down to Virginia was that the money I transferred to him I "owed" to him for making his first visit so difficult.

Yet, here I was. Meeting up with him and spending the day with him. Think my logic a bit twisted, but there was just something about him that honestly made me kind of thrilled to see him again.

Shamari came to my hotel on a Friday afternoon and we spent the entire day together. And honestly, we had a wonderful time. He was once again charming and funny and he stayed with me till nightfall. And here I was again, not wanting him to leave.

Later that evening though, we were sitting side-by-side on the bed watching TV. I have a habit in which I bite my nails and sometimes do it unintentionally and without really realizing I'm doing it.

41

He was holding my hand and caressing it and then suddenly took a long hard look at it.

"Why would you bite your nails?" he asked. "You know when you bite your nails, it means you're nervous."

"Oh, sorry, no I always bite my nails," I replied. "I actually do it out of habit sometimes and have done it since I was a little girl."

Adamant in wanting to prove *his* point, he then grabbed his phone and began Googling 'nail-biting as a symptom of nervousness or stress.'

"Here," he pointed out rather smugly. "You have a nervous condition, it says! That's probably why you're so crazy too." Before letting out what sounded like self-satisfied laughter.

I admit, I didn't know how to respond to that. Not until what he said next which rendered me completely speechless.

"And now that I look at it, you have ugly hands!" he said bluntly.

I went dead silent. Yes, maybe biting one's nails is a rather odd or maybe even gross habit to some, but I didn't understand his reaction. And I was clueless as to why he'd say such a thing. He's never criticized my outward appearance before. And I'm sorry, Shamari; you don't have any disgusting or annoying habits yourself?

42

But then, he apologized and did everything in his will the remainder of the evening to cheer me up and make up for what he said. He was being cute again, and what was so difficult was that I gave in.

"I will come back tomorrow and stay with you, okay?" he said softly before kissing my cheek.

I was once again feeling bliss, *almost* as if what he said earlier didn't even happen. But it wasn't like I completely forgot and put it out of my mind and dismissed it as simply Shamari having "a moment." I stayed up a bit longer, TV on in the background still, and just stared at my hands. I think I may have actually stared at my hands until I fell asleep.

First thing the next morning I went to a salon to get a manicure. Since I felt so strongly about what Shamari said, I only got the manicure because what he said really hurt my self-esteem. But I also thought, it probably would have been a nice surprise for him for when he'd meet me at the hotel at around 5:00 pm.

I left the salon feeling a little better about myself and thought, well maybe this was better for me after all. Maybe it was time that I took even more care of my appearance.

I then heard an alert on my phone. I received a direct message, hoping it was Shamari, but no. It was a message that crushed me and grinded me almost to dust.

It was a random girl, saying that she too was having sex with Shamari.

"Who in the world...?" I said out loud, completely stuttering and unsure how to react at that moment, especially since I was in public and surrounded by the typical waves of big city crowds ambling to and from work, running errands, and so forth. "He was just here last night telling me that he loved me!"

I called Shamari immediately, which he didn't answer, and texted him as well and told him to call me back right away; that I needed to talk to him because it was urgent. He texted back and asked if I was okay.

'You need to call me RIGHT NOW!!!' I wrote in my text.

He called instantly and asked what was going on. I told him about the message. Shamari then sounded very casual and said very nonchalantly that he knew who it was.

"Who is she, Shamari!" I demanded a quick and direct explanation.

"It's a girl who's stalking me," he replied. "She is mad because I won't accept her friend or follow requests on Facebook. She's doing this to my other female friends as well. She's just a jealous person!"

For my peace of mind, he forwarded other messages; conversations he's had with his other female friends notifying him that this same woman was sending similar messages to *them*.

I quickly calmed down, since I saw the proof and gave him the benefit of the doubt. I got off the phone with him because he said he had to go back to work.

As it got closer to 5:00 pm, I texted Shamari to tell him I was dressed and ready to go out to dinner. He replied with a simple, *'Ok.'*

Then…it was 6:00 pm and he was still a no-show. I called him and I was sent straight to voicemail.

No! I was NOT going to put up with that that night! I kept calling and calling and did so till he answered. I had a sinking feeling he was never at work that day, that something else was going on, and he was once again planning on ghosting me.

Finally, I annoyed him enough to where he answered and I was shocked at what came out of his mouth.

45

"M_____ f_____! Stop calling my phone!" he screamed and then hung up.

I was mortified, feeling rejected once again. The devil was really pouring it on. I felt the Holy Spirit move through me, really encouraging me to walk away; and convincing me Satan was just baiting and provoking me.

I was shattered yet again and was beyond hurt that Shamari would say that to me. And call me that! And then suddenly kick me to the side like crumpled, balled-up paper on the sidewalk that got in his way. A girlfriend I knew up there came to my hotel and sat with me for a while; consoling me even though I was disconsolate and completely inconsolable that night.

I was, in my own very twisted way, still crazy about him. Looking back, I cannot comprehend why but even though I felt messed up inside, it wasn't enough to let go and give up on him. It should've been easy. Leaving for good when he said that to me should've been a given. The Spirit I know was throwing every sign at me telling me to leave him alone. This is not a man who God has for you; I could hear the Spirit say. Stop playing with fire! This man is a demon!

But I didn't want to let go. He was my addiction. My body craved his touch, all the while clinging to the false hope that he could legitimately fall in love with me and we'd live happily ever after. So, I kept ignoring the signs. I kept ignoring God.

"How much do you want to bet he wasn't even at work today," my friend said.

I told her about this other woman that messaged me and flat-out told me she was having sex with Shamari. My girlfriend then tried hard to convince me he was probably with her all along and to get away from Shamari and leave him be. That he was awful and he was getting me offtrack with God.

But all I could say was that I loved him too much and it was just too difficult to let go.

He had me right where he wanted me.

8

I woke up one morning and made a promise to myself. I wasn't going to let my desires and my obsession with Shamari take me over.

Three months passed after coming back from New York and I was so proud of myself for having no contact with him. I felt a sense of relief not giving into the temptation of sending a text or Facebook message. As a matter of fact, during those three months I even joined a support group that would help really put into perspective Shamari's behavior. I came to the realization that he was suffering from narcissistic personality disorder and the support group really helped me understand narcissistic behaviors, the signs, the short-term and long-term consequences, etc.

Comprehending the characteristics of narcissism helped me reevaluate my situation with Shamari. I couldn't be more grateful for the support group as well as the many video lectures discussing the traits of a narcissist and what they're capable of. People's personal testimonies

I watched online were also real eye-openers. It helped me understand what I was dealing with and it was comforting to know and see I wasn't the only one.

It did help me reclaim my confidence but only for another three months until all of a sudden, and completely out of the blue, I found myself missing him again. I couldn't shake the positive memories of our deep, meaningful conversations during the beginning of our relationship. I couldn't get over missing the side of Shamari that made me fall in love with him like this. The one thing narcissists are good at is making you miss them even when there's nothing to miss, but believing there was a softer, gentler side of him, I couldn't stop asking myself, "What if?"

But the aching and longing returned and got so intense to the point that I did the unthinkable...I actually called him. Hearing his voice again made me do a one-eighty back in the opposite direction, but I didn't care. I was happy to hear his voice again. His spell just couldn't be broken.

I told this devil, Shamari, I wanted to be the one to love him, even though I knew the kind of person he was. But inside I did have to acknowledge him for who he really was, and he was indeed the devil. Or how I'd imagine the devil to be. But I just couldn't break these chains. He had a hold I struggle to this day to put into words!

We again kept in contact. I traveled and made a few more trips to New York. I would call him to my hotel rooms and he would stay with me throughout my visits. And yes, we'd have sex. I felt like I was in heaven not even thinking about the fact I was letting my faith slowly deteriorate and I was doing things well against my personal beliefs just to satisfy my hunger. At that moment, I was sleeping with the devil disregarding all the horrible things he's done and said to me.

There was a time I went to New York City on a church trip to partake in different activities held at the church that involved praise, worship, and outreach. But then, the devil reared his ugly head and talked to me in his most alluring way to deflect me from my mission and what I went there to do, "Hey baby, you just going to leave me here by myself?"

I was hoping for some sort of compromise and I tried to get him involved somehow since when we first got to know each other, he seemed so on fire for God.

"Why don't you come with me?" I asked. "We can do these activities together."

He declined. But then he was able to convince me to ditch my outreach altogether to be with him. I willingly participated in the devil's game, dropping my plans to do what I promised God I would do in His house. His place of worship.

It was sinful of me to do what I did. To ignore His message. To neglect Him and ignore His effort to save me from a wretch like Shamari. I was lusting after the devil and couldn't quash my intense desires. Like being in a committed relationship or a long-term marriage only to readily risk jeopardizing it to satisfy my lusts with a newer, hotter, and younger model. The temptation was too much and it ultimately trapped and consumed me.

This demon had gotten such a tight hold on me that when it was time to return home, I didn't want to leave. I had sunk so far deep I couldn't swim my way to the surface anymore no matter how hard I tried. All I could think about was him. He *was* my every thought. I couldn't leave him alone now.

It was just one month later; I returned to New York to get involved in more church-related activities. Again, I tried so hard and promised myself I wasn't going to call him; or that at least I would try to be more involved with what I actually went there to do. I wasn't going to invite him to the hotel this time. But once I got there, a couple of hours passed before I found myself calling him to let him know I was in town. Shamari then told me he wouldn't be able see me that first night but the next one would work, which only deepened the anticipation. I was yearning for the devil's flesh, an all-consuming passion and desire to have him with me. But the remainder of that trip was a repeat of the last. Going on these trips for ministry was purely just an excuse to be with him.

New Year's Eve came and I called Shamari to ask if he would come be with me for the holiday because I wanted to spend it with someone. When he agreed, it felt special. I felt special.

He had assured me he'd be by earlier that afternoon, but it was now past dusk and he still hadn't shown up nor was there any word from him. I was let down yet again, so certain that I was being stood up once more. And I was right back to furiously reaching out to him to tell him off.

"I'm on my way!" he insisted. "Just give me time!"

"You said you'd be here earlier and it is now night!" I fired back. "Just don't come!"

I was completely frustrated and felt that this would be a completely wasted trip. What am I doing, I thought? I can't go on like this!

But then just several minutes later, I got an incoming call from Shamari.

"Call me a Lyft, I'm ready for you now baby," he said kindly, as if everything from moments ago once again never occurred.

And just like that, the switch flipped and I was happy again. I stared at the Lyft tracker as his car was approaching. I felt like a teenager again, awaiting my first date with the boy I'd had a crush on almost all school year.

He arrived at the hotel, looking good and wearing the cologne I liked. Shamari knew exactly what to do to make himself irresistible to me and I hated it, but loved it simultaneously. The devil knows your weaknesses. He knows what makes you vulnerable. And I fell for it every time and most times without hesitation.

Every time I was traveling up specifically for church events, he would always persuade me to be with him and spend time with him instead. That man of faith never even existed, but I didn't care. There were days I did go to the church functions but then once they were done, I immediately ran right back to him. Later, he was able to convince me to skip them entirely. He got in my head, but I didn't mind at the time. I wasn't going to turn down something that felt too good to me and made me feel alive.

Shamari kept telling me how much he loved me. And would always tell me he missed me whenever I was away. I was blinded by his looks, his touch, and the way he held me. I was a blind woman walking without a cane or a guide dog, but for me it didn't matter as long as I walked that straight line that led to him. I loved what I felt and wanted to feel that way forever.

It was the new year, and I was in a strong, healthy sexual relationship. I told him how much I loved him and he would always tell me he loved me back even though he didn't mean it.

What I felt for him made me ignore everything else. It made me ignore all the signs telling me he was totally wrong for me and what he was doing was just to lead me astray. But it was also my choice to ignore them.

Shamari was a snake that hypnotized his prey. I didn't care at what lengths I went to, to be with him. We went out to eat and I paid for everything and didn't mind if it was what I had to do to keep him around. To keep him by my side.

Even when he would diss me and make me feel stupid or worthless. Make me feel like the smallest person on earth. And always I could never do right in his eyes. He had a hold on me that I wasn't willing to let go. Even when I couldn't understand how he could be so thankless and at times hostile; I showed him so much love regardless of it all.

9

I went to mind-boggling lengths to please him. I bought him clothes, shoes, and hats. I sent money basically whenever he asked or when he swindled me out of it. I paid for hotels but didn't care as long as I had him with me.

He always made me feel loved even though I knew then the whole thing was a façade. He put on whatever act he could to get what he wanted out of me. But I loved him dearly and my love was authentic. He only loved me when he wanted money, clothes, food, and sex. But I didn't care because I was addicted to him.

I spent New Year's 2021 with him; doing all the things I wanted with him to ring in the new year. But knowing in how much danger I was because he was so toxic and dangerous, I had to realize eventually he was truly wrong for me and find a way to break loose. It had been two years and I knew this "relationship" was going nowhere.

When it was time to go home, I missed him as much as I always missed him whenever I had to leave. I thought about him the entire plane ride home, though I knew deep in my heart he wasn't thinking about me at all. But I think that day that's when it really hit me. He was unapologetically a bad person. A user, a liar, and a selfish egomaniac and cheat. A manipulator that always found a way to make me feel sorry for him. To feel an incredible amount of sympathy though everything that came out of his mouth was a lie.

I was easily fooled. I constantly felt punched in the gut by him but was too hopelessly in love to make him stop. He got clothes, food, money, and free hotel stays, always claiming he was in financial dire straits. But I knew he was full of it. I fully acknowledged it all wasn't true. Then again, he knew I would spend my money just because it was *him*. The devil in Armani!

All the way up to the middle of January, I kept telling him how much I loved him, missed him, and wanted badly for the two of us to be together and he'd say he felt the same but rarely showed it. He'd say anything because he knew I was one of his "suppliers." Someone who supplies him with everything he needs whenever he needs it. Somebody who gives and gives and gives and gets zilch in return. And I often wondered what number woman I was. His fourth, fifth, twelfth on the side maybe?

57

For all I know, this monster probably was legally married and had some more kids out there I didn't know about.

He knew exactly how to play his cards right and always showed his best poker face. Seek out and target those that are vulnerable and keep them lined neatly on his shelf. People like him know exactly who they can play and they use whatever they can to their advantage without feeling a sliver of remorse. Devoid of conscience was used to describe them at my support group.

I was beginning to feel uneasy the moment I purchased my ticket to New York City. Something was off and I felt the Spirit work through me, letting me know I was in for a ruder awakening.

When I got there, I found out he was with another woman he claimed to be his housemate. It was obvious she wasn't, especially when I was only allowed to call him and see him on specific times of the day.

He stubbornly denied and flat-out lied about his infidelities...to me and to these other women apparently. But as emotional as I was, because it was him, I left the whole thing alone and just let it be as it was and cried in silence.

It was just a mere two weeks after I returned home and I was already dying to see him again. I yearned to be with him so much, I couldn't stop crying infinite tears of frustration. What was this hold the devil had on me? Why did I feel so powerless to such a soulless coward? I didn't *want* him with me...I *needed* him with me. So much so that not long after my return, I purchased a roundtrip airline ticket for him as well as a hotel room. His visit to Virginia I made sure would be extra special.

We had communicated consistently from the time I purchased his ticket to the day before his arrival. We had been counting down the days together and he convinced me just how excited he was to see me and how thrilled he was to get away. The night before his departure from Newark International, he said to me he was completely packed and ready to go.

The day of his arrival came and I got dressed in my finest to make sure I looked my best for him when I picked him up from the airport.

He was flying United, which was departing Newark at 12:16 pm.

Then, something began to feel off. The feeling was odd and I don't quite know how to describe what it was, but something wasn't right.

59

I called the service desk in Newark around 11:30 am to see if he had boarded the plane yet. The agent, a companionable and patient-sounding lady, informed me that the passenger hadn't yet boarded, but that he still had another 30 minutes now due to a 15-minute departure delay.

My heart began pounding. I just knew something was about to happen. After the scheduled departure of his flight, I then decided to call the agent back.

"Sorry ma'am, he was the only passenger that didn't check in and the flight is already enroute to Dulles," she said.

My heart dropped to my stomach like a rock. I immediately broke down in the middle of the airport in front of the flight information display system. I wasted my money. Both the flight and hotel non-refundable. I called and called him and no answer. Nothing! I texted and texted and told him off again, saying the same harsh angry words whenever he stood me up without a care. I got zero response. But I made it abundantly clear that I never wanted to see him again. It was over!

With the hotel room being non-refundable and, in my name, I decided to just get away and use the room for myself for a bit of a staycation; although I was just not in the mood.

I was lying in bed and five hours later I got a voicemail alert on my phone. I had blocked him everywhere I possibly could, so when he tried to call, he was sent straight to voicemail.

He said in a very distressed manner that he was locked up. That he had gotten into a fight and urged me to call him as soon as possible. He was very apologetic, but this time I didn't fall for it and I didn't call him back.

Instead, I decided to call the Hudson County Jail. I gave them Shamari's full name and asked if there was anyone taken into custody by that name. The officer told me that no one was brought in under that name.

"Anyone arrested in Jersey City, would they be taken to *this* jail?" I asked for clarification.

"Yes ma'am," the officer replied.

Come to find out Shamari was unable to get away from his so-called roommate. That was the real deal, the reason why he missed his flight.

I also planned to surprise him with an all-expenses paid trip for his birthday and was able to cancel those reservations without penalty. I was so mad and hurt but I wasn't surprised anymore. I had just coped with the fact that this was just the kind of stuff he did and this was the real him.

10

It also didn't surprise me that falling out of love with him wouldn't be easy. The trip for his birthday was a five-star resort that I could barely afford. I had zero control at this point that it wasn't going to be easy to break from the devil's grip. I was still stark raving mad about a delusional psychopath that didn't care about me one bit. A man that did everything in his power to take advantage of vulnerable women because he knew he could get away with it.

It was the beginning of February that he reached out to me and yes, you guessed it, I was right back to where I started. I realized I missed him so much that I was happy again to hear his voice. I was still in love. And I wasn't going anywhere.

He then told me he was now considering moving down to Virginia. Oh boy! So, without a second thought I helped him look for rooms for rent and even offered to pay the first month's because I just wanted to be close to him and knew money would be tight for him. I was also making the move in looking for places to live myself, but I *was* being smart about it and wasn't going to allow myself to do something insane like move in with him...so I thought.

While talking to him over the phone the very next day, he then asked me to come get him immediately.

"What do you mean, come get you?" I asked, extremely puzzled.

"Come pick me up," said Shamari. "I want to be with you *now*. I love you and I miss you."

"Shamari, I'm living back at home now," I said. My adrenaline shot up because I was getting nervous how all this was going to even be possible. I wanted to go and pick him up and bring him here, but I didn't know how that was going to be a realistic possibility. "I no longer live in my apartment. I *am* looking for a place though. I have an appointment soon to take a tour of one that's becoming available in three weeks."

"That's okay then. Come get me when you move in, okay?"

"Are you sure you wanna come here to be with me, Shamari?"

"Yes! As long as you are sure you want me to be a part of your life," he said.

(Never mind what I said earlier about not moving in with him!)

"Well...yes," I replied reluctantly. "If you are truly sure this is what you want!"

"Yes! I want to be with you," he said.

Then, I couldn't believe the words that came out of my mouth next.

"You know what, Shamari? Why don't I just get you now? It's okay. We don't have to wait three weeks."

"Really?" he said. "But where am I going to stay?"

"Don't worry. I'll pay for a hotel."

"Thank you, baby. Just come up to Jersey and pick me up if you are sure about all this. Only if it isn't hard for you or too much to ask."

"It'll be fine," I said. "I can come Saturday or Sunday."

"Monday would be better actually," said Shamari.

"Why can't I come up during the weekend?" I asked. That coming Monday was a holiday but I preferred the weekend especially since I had to be back at work early on Tuesday.

"No. I have some things to do before I leave so Monday will be better, please."

Her, I thought! He was spending the weekend with her—the "roommate." That's why. But did I care? Of course not! Because he was going to be with me. He'd be far away from her. And he'd be all mine.

I booked the hotel for him that Monday. It was hard to get any sleep that night so I got up at 3:30 am and just went ahead and got ready to go.

I was out the door and on the road by 4:15, which avoided much of the DC-area traffic, thank goodness. He called to check up on me from time to time while I was on the road and I lit up every time I heard his voice. He was making sure I was okay and being a caring, considerate gentleman.

The whole way there I started to consider the possibility that maybe Shamari was coming to Virginia to start over, work on himself, and try and change for the better and for me. I saw some change in him already (yes, even though he was still with this other woman that weekend). But all I could think about was how I'd see him every day. I'd be with him every day and he would be all mine; no one else's. You probably know where this is going, but me being so blind I couldn't predict what was actually to come.

I got to his house and rain, sleet, and freezing rain had begun to descend upon the city. I arrived at his place late that morning and he was standing in the garage with all his things packed and ready to be loaded. We hugged each other tightly and immediately started putting his things in my car.

He was so sweet, so warm and cordial that day. I was convinced that he had truly changed. I felt at that moment he genuinely loved me and cared about me. I was on top of the world and beyond because Shamari was now with me and we were official and we'd always be together. Just us.

We got on the road early that afternoon and didn't get back to Virginia until late that evening. During the road trip, he received a call from what I presumed was the roommate (or exes or others on the side, who knows). But I remained silent. I didn't say anything to him when he got off the phone. It didn't matter anymore because whoever she was, she was now in the past.

He reached over and took my hand and said with softness in his eyes, "Why don't people want me to be happy? Especially with the woman I love and that loves me back?"

It warmed my heart to hear him say that. He had to have changed, I thought. This is the new him! He drove almost the whole way back so I could rest. We joked. Sang along to songs we had on, on the stereo. And we just talked. Talked like we talked the first year we got to know each other. I was in heaven again.

At one point during the drive down, he said, "Thank you for coming to get me and to be with me. Please, let's not have what happened the last time happen again. Let's try to get along this time. Let's start over."

11

I stressed to Shamari that if ever something bothered us, we really needed to take an amicable approach and work through it always with patience, maturity, and civility. We organized some kind of verbal relationship agreement before we decided to embark on this journey together. The journey as an official, cohabitating couple.

We arrived at the hotel later that evening and were exhausted from the drive. We unpacked and took all his belongings to the room.

Suddenly, I really started to feel the higher powers move through me, practically screaming their message. Something was off; way off! Something still wasn't right, despite that Shamari seemed sincere about wanting to start all over again and have a new beginning with me. This wasn't about genuine love, honesty, and loyalty. This wasn't about getting in a serious relationship or eventually getting married. It was about my feelings of lust and infatuation disguising themselves as things they weren't. Over and over, I ignored God. Over and over, I deliberately wrote off the red flags. Shamari's flesh felt good against mine. His touch, his kiss; the sex felt just good, which underscored even more the fact that this relationship was built on a foundation of superficialities. Yet, since it had been so long since I had anything physical, it was what I needed more than anything else. And not just his touch and his kiss. But also, to say sweet things to me even if he only said it because he just wanted to get his way. My body hungered. It yearned for this demon.

We had the hotel for three weeks until my apartment was finally ready to move into. I loved being able to be with him at the end of the day every day, but during this time, he had grown completely aloof and indifferent.

He was gaming all day long and only sporadically acknowledged my presence. He was glued to the gaming system and preferred to interact with the players on that game far more than he was willing to interact with me. All he wanted to do the preponderance of time was to play his online game versus giving an ounce of attention to me like he promised. I guess he defined "being together" as being in the same space but doing different things. Like we were an old married couple living our final years in peaceful indifference; him having his side of the room and me having mine. Him playing a game on his phone or handheld console on his side of the bed while I read a book on mine; with an impenetrable and unbreakable invisible wall between us.

I told him this wasn't what I meant by spending time together. But there it was again! He got defensive and completely snapped. I ran into the bathroom after we had an explosive argument, sobbing almost uncontrollably, especially when he shut me down with, "F___ you! Leave me alone!"

Now, the Holy Spirit was just shaking His head and rolling His eyes! I heard Him say, plainly to me, "Why are you crying?" with a voice that almost seemed derisive. "This is who you wanted, right? This is what you wanted, wasn't it?"

I cried even more because I knew what I was doing was hurting God and pulling me further and further away from Him. I knew I was making some very horrible mistakes that I would come to regret and that would bite me in the end. I knew I was in the wrong for allowing this so-called "relationship" to go the lengths it did even though it didn't have a snowball's chance in you know where.

71

Shamari and I had more than several major quarrels similar to the one we had that night. All of which centered around Shamari's neglect. I'd come out of the bathroom and he'd remain uncaring; totally distant and apathetic. But he was confident. He was confident I wouldn't put my foot down and throw him out. He was confident I wouldn't storm out myself. And to be perfectly honest, he had every right to feel that way, because I was the one that gave him that confidence. I was the pawn in his evil game. He knew there was nothing he could say that would chase me away because I'd always come running back.

The thing about narcissists is that the narcissist lacks all feelings of compassion and empathy. And sometimes they're totally sadistic. They love to see you hurt. They love to see you suffer and they are openly mentally-cruel. They get a sick high off torturing you emotionally.

The next morning after one of our discords from the night before, he walked me to my car as he'd done almost every morning.

"Have a blessed day, baby," he said very kindly before kissing me softly, once again as if nothing happened.

I returned home from work that day and he was again gaming online. I kissed him after entering the room and setting my stuff down. But this time, he wasn't having an off-day. He was in a much better mood, and actually seemed really happy.

"Did you have a good day?" he asked.

"Yes," I told him, relieved he wasn't being the Shamari he was the previous night. "I had a wonderful day," I added.

"You wanna go get something to eat? Maybe around five or six?" he asked.

"Sure."

"I want something different."

"Well...there's a good all-you-can-eat place I know of that we can go to."

"Sounds good. We can go there, baby."

We went to the buffet and he loved it. We had a quiet evening for once. And it made things feel normal. It made *us* feel normal. And he even paid for dinner, which shocked me since I got used to paying for everything.

Then, in the following days he showed interest in me again. He wanted to spend more time with me.

"What do you wanna do today?" asked Shamari.

"Why don't we watch a movie together and have some popcorn," I suggested.

He graciously agreed and like a *real* couple we laid in bed and watched a movie and talked. Then, after the movie we played the game Battleship. We played three rounds and he won all three, but it was calming just spending this time with him.

The next day, I texted him from work and asked what he wanted to do that evening. No answer. I didn't receive a response all day, which worried me again.

I got back to the room and he was back on that stupid game! Not once breaking from it to even respond to my message. But—he was still calm and I didn't make any sort of fuss about him not answering my text since I was afraid it could set him off. He turned off the game and we decided to go to the mall. It was a normal evening again, spending time together as we have had the nights before.

But then…as we were on our way back home, there was a car pulling into the street in front of us and I wasn't sure if Shamari was paying attention to it or not. I said calmly, "Hey Shamari, watch out for that car."

Then, he quickly got very irate, pulled the car over, and came to an almost screeching halt.

"You drive then if think I'm blind or something!" he yelled.

"Why are you so upset?" I asked, now fearing for my safety. "I was only making sure you saw the car."

"You clearly think I'm blind or something!" he basically screamed. "If you wanna take control of the wheel, you drive the car then!"

This snowballed into another major blowout in the hotel room and we had perhaps one of our worst arguments yet.

I called my two girlfriends, Lynette and Patricia, and told them what happened.

Shamari then yelled, "You're just another dumb m____ f_____! Just leave me the f___ alone!"

I told Lynette and Patricia I was leaving the hotel that night and going back to family. I stopped by the front desk at the hotel and told the receptionist I didn't want the room anymore past that coming Wednesday, which meant Shamari had only three days to get out.

The apartment wouldn't be ready until that Friday, but I wasn't waiting a day longer and I didn't care what Shamari did at that point. He had three whole days to figure it out.

Lynette and Patricia convinced me and convinced me NOT to go back to him. Let him be and let that dog find his own way back home; and hopefully back to New Jersey or anywhere else far, far away.

I was so upset and hurt. This was the worst he's made me feel yet. I sobbed and wept with so much pain in my heart.

Lynette and Patricia did everything in their will to calm me down and said so many positive and uplifting things to me.

BUT! By next morning when I finally calmed down, I began feeling very bad for him and guilty for canceling the room. He would be alone and had nowhere to go. He knew no one in Virginia except me.

So, when I got to work, I texted him again and asked if there was any chance we could talk it through. He later responded and agreed it would be best. On the text, he said this in a way that gave me the impression we could discuss this affably. Plus, I hated doing this to him and always had the bad habit of being kind to those who aren't kind to me. My girlfriends warned me that if I went back to him, they'd kick my butt. I laughed when they said that even though they were only half-joking.

I already knew I was going back to him no matter what. That's just what I did.

12

I headed to the hotel right after work, expecting Shamari to be the calmer person the text suggested. Wrong!

The moment I entered the room he immediately blew up at me.

"WHY DID YOU GO TO THE FRONT DESK AND CHANGE THE DAYS!? F____ YOU! What was I supposed to do, huh!? Live on the streets!? You know I don't know no one here! You know that! This was your plan all along! You brought me here to do this to me! To leave me high and dry, huh!"

"You agreed to come here!" I yelled back. "Don't put this all on me! You called me a m____ f____ and made me feel horrible about myself, so I was hurt! I was mad at you! That's why I did it!"

"To hell with you! I'm renting a U-Haul and going back to Jersey! This is all your fault! This is all your fault, Nikki!"

Never once did he reflect his own actions. Never once did he apologize and take even a shred of responsibility. That psychotic narcissist only saw what I had done. Not why I did it. It would somehow be my fault no matter what.

But I needed desperately for this situation to not reach past its boiling point, so I did the only thing I knew to do then and there: take the blame, apologize, and beg, not ask, but beg for his forgiveness. Then I went back to the hotel clerk and asked him to change the dates back to the original reservation.

I ran back to him and I told Lynette and Patricia. "No! No! NO!" Lynette almost shouted. "Don't you know you deserve so much better, Nikki? Don't you know you're above this? Think of your self-worth! Value yourself, Nikki!"

But no matter what my friends said, it didn't make a difference. It didn't change anything because I still loved him. But then my friends asked questions that, to be completely honest, stumped me. Questions that didn't have a clear answer.

"Seriously. What is it that you love about him?" asked Patricia.

"What could you possibly love about him? What is there to love, Nikki? He doesn't know how to love others. Only himself," said Lynette.

They were very good questions. Questions I couldn't answer because I had no answer. So, all I could do was come up with a weak, cop-out response in perhaps the most cowardly fashion a woman could when trying to find excuses to defend her boyfriend's abuse.

"I understand what you're saying. But deep down he really means no harm, and in my heart, *I* truly love him. And that's all that matters."

Shamari was only pretending to cry at this point because he knew his crocodile tears would work. And they did.

The next day was my appointment to look at the apartment. I asked if he wanted to accompany me and he said yes.

We got there and I just kept hearing that voice telling me that what I was doing was absolutely stupid and my biggest mistake yet. That this situation was shaming me in the eyes of God and I knew it but was letting it happen anyway. Once again, I disregarded that voice and the feelings that came with it. I was about to be with the man that I loved and was still convinced that with us living together he would see just how much I loved him and that would change him wholly for the better.

I kept telling myself, it will be better because I will get to see him every day. It's going to be wonderful having someone to come home to and talk to. I didn't have to chat with him via FaceTime or phone; he would be right there with me. My boyfriend. The one that belonged to me. And that would make things better. Maybe everything he'd been through back in New York and New Jersey took a toll on him mentally and emotionally. Maybe lack of stability and feeling out of place was a trigger—and that everything would be settled once we lived together and our relationship would give him a sense of purpose. And besides, no relationship is perfect, right?

After the tour of the apartment was complete, we went out to look for things we would need for the new place before we had dinner together and called it a night. Things were okay the remainder of the day and I would strive to make sure we had more days like that one if I could help it.

Now came move-in day. It was the First of March and we were unloading our things into the new apartment. I couldn't get a U-Haul until that coming Saturday so we had to sleep on the floor for two nights.

Because of this move with Shamari, my relationships with family and friends soured. My family was upset. My kids barely spoke to me. My friends were getting beyond frustrated with me for not leaving him. It felt surreal but it didn't bother me that much because I thought this was the right thing to do. I was with Shamari and it was us against the world.

Saturday came and we went to pick up the moving truck early that morning. On the way to the U-Haul rental facility, Shamari told me he needed coffee.

"Sure. We'll stop at a Starbucks once we get close to the lot," I said, not thinking this would upset him.

Suddenly...

"Why does everything got to be YOUR way!" he exclaimed angrily. "It's going to be a long day and I need coffee NOW!"

"Shamari, it's okay, calm down," I said very soothingly, trying everything at that moment to quickly settle him down like a mother to a screaming child. "I'm going to stop somewhere once we get closer. You act like I flat-out told you no."

"Whatever! You don't listen! You never listen! Seriously! What is wrong with you!" he lashed out.

With my intense willingness to make this work to both our advantages, I caved and just pulled into the nearest McDonald's so he could have his coffee.

Afterwards, we pressed on and he remained dead silent. He didn't say thank you or anything. I said nothing more to him either on the way to the lot.

We entered the U-Haul facility and stood in line. He knew how shaken and upset I was by his outburst. Shamari then tried to comfort me but I wouldn't say much to him. He then gave up and went back to the car and waited.

After retrieving the moving truck, we then headed to storage to get my furniture and other belongings. My son came to help even though he didn't want to be in Shamari's presence at all. A coworker of mine also came to help as well as Lynette, even though she thought I was making the worst decision of my life.

Loading and unloading was a long and arduous process, but we got everything done in one day.

Shamari helped unload the heavy items into the house and even though I offered my assistance he insisted he got it and told me nicely not to worry. I told him how appreciative I was of him.

Shamari got a lot accomplished that evening. The living room was organized and put together as well as the bedroom. He called me in to ask for my opinion and if I was happy with the set-up. I told him I liked everything the way it was and that he did a terrific job with both rooms. I organized the kitchen and the bathroom. Finally, it felt like home.

Later that night, we went to Walmart for some additional items and necessities. Shamari bought a microwave as well as groceries, hangers for all our clothes, a broom, mop, and other cleaning supplies. At that moment, everything felt just right. It seemed as if Shamari was now settled, and I convinced myself that the stress of moving and the fact he's not a morning person was the reason for his outburst on our way to U-Haul. I wanted to convince myself of that anyway.

But as you know, this next stage would completely and ultimately disillusion me. All the warning signs I got before would truly prove making things work with Shamari was a wasted effort. How everything he said and did was a lie, but that also I totally lied to myself. God kept telling me to run. Let go and stay away from him. But I didn't want to hear it. I wanted so badly to think in my alternate reality that this could work somehow and I could be with him forever. But what could've been definitely wasn't meant to be as I was absolutely in love with evil. And that evil would be unleashed in even worse ways than before.

13

My bible was locked in the trunk of my car. Just sitting there collecting dust. I always felt I was being communicated to through scripture but I made a choice. Either read my bible and accept the Word of God in my heart and make the right choices in life and in love. Or, keep my bible hidden away and continue sleeping with the enemy to keep feeding into some far-fetched fantasy that this relationship was actually going to go the distance.

It would be difficult to call Shamari by his name. He was Satan! And I was so enticed and spellbound by this demon that was weakening me by the second.

There was nothing this monster could do that could chase me away. There was no act terrible enough that would make me turn in the other direction. I was in my own version of hell and I was about to be damned for all eternity. And it was getting to the point that I was much lonelier with him than I was without, but I couldn't let go.

Everything was his way or no way. His definition of spending time with me was now running simple errands together and being in the same apartment (even when we were in separate rooms). I asked a coworker of mine if I was crazy for trying to make it work with him.

She said I wasn't crazy for just simply wanting to make my relationship work, but then proceeded to offer valuable advice. I put her on speakerphone so Shamari could hear, but he was glued to his online game, not paying attention at all to what she was saying. He didn't work. As a matter of fact, he collected unemployment from New York. He was now only pretending in our relationship and I felt totally lost.

After me and my coworker got off the phone, the devil was unleashed, going off on me and cussing me out making accusations that I intentionally sabotaged him and ruined his life. He called me crazy and other things I dare not repeat. Said I was the sick one. And told me *I* was the one that needed help. Mr. Know-It-All! Giving himself credit where credit obviously wasn't due. His hypocrisy was unbelievable and I couldn't understand how one of the most calculating human beings I've ever met was trying to tell me *I* needed the help, but that he was the perfect one!

Then, he started taking ownership of and splitting everything. The demon now took total ownership of the possessions he bought. He ordered me not to touch any of the food in the fridge that I didn't pay for and that if I wanted any of it, I would have to go to the store and buy my own (or pay him for it). And I did just that.

I started cooking for myself now since we were not allowed to share anything he bought with "his" money. It blew my mind, but I walked right into it believing that somehow this demon could be fixed.

I lost myself. I lost my identity. I lost everything that was me and started realizing my choices, my decisions, and my life now revolved around this monster. And on top of that, he freely put me down and insulted me whenever he felt like it. He even began punishing me. He told me because I was so crazy and needy, he was no longer going to give me sex until I knew how to act right. He even told me that I was the toxic one and I was the one bringing *him* down.

Everything that I felt about him. Everything that was happening to me—he tried to turn it around and say I was doing it to *him*! Like HE was the victim!

"You know? I don't care if you withhold sex from me. That doesn't bother me one bit," I said to him, since his behavior was such a turn off that I couldn't get myself to be attracted to him anymore anyway.

"You see? And that's why you're crazy! You're the one going to a therapist! You don't see me going to one! You're the crazy one, Nikki!" he hit back.

"I am nowhere near as crazy as you! I go to my therapist to help me with my trust issues! Because of people like you who lie and cheat and manipulate! You are a narcissist, Shamari! And *you're* the one that needs help whether you want to see it or not!"

"You don't even know what a narcissist is!" he said, condescendingly and defensively. "You don't know what a narcissist is because you are so stupid!"

"Look in the mirror! And you'll see what a narcissist looks like!"

I pondered what we actually were together endlessly that night and got to thinking while sitting there and just watching him, while he wasn't even acknowledging my existence. I remembered him saying something to me when I first met him. When I first saw shades of darkness in him.

He said so boldly, "You don't really know who you are talking to, do you?"

As those words came out his mouth, I could hear the voice of the devil speaking to me so clearly.

Within, I recognized who I was talking to and the kind of person I was dealing with, but I convinced myself he was too kind, too sweet of a man, and he didn't really mean anything by what he said when he said that. I truly believed this was the man God was sending to me. But after we moved in together, I said, "No way!"

Coming back to the present, it was a Sunday night and we were sitting on the sofa. His phone was lying between us. He glanced over at it and then at me and said to me very intensely, "You know, I could call a few people and let you talk to them and they could tell you some really bad things that I did to them. But just know if I do anything to hurt you, it's only because I love you."

"What? Do you plan to hurt me?" I asked this monster, confused and almost terrified. "This is scary for real! Would you actually physically hurt me?"

He said nothing.

I couldn't sleep that whole night. I locked my bedroom door since he was sleeping on the sofa. When he banned us from having sex as part of my "punishment," he decided to sleep in the living room.

I think we only slept together two nights right after we moved into the apartment before he decided we needed to sleep in separate rooms. He neither wanted to have sex nor give me any kind of attention until I learned my lesson. His love didn't exist—because there was never any love there. I was always about him and what he wanted and he aimed to keep it that way.

He made me fear him constantly because he was a ticking bomb. The love-bombing became a nuclear device that would detonate and level everything in its path. I was afraid to say anything. Afraid that I would say something that would trigger him because he would just go off unexpectedly on me. And sometimes his rage was unmanageable. And now, I had to also be afraid that he could beat me up as well. Maybe even kill me.

14

"I wanna be the one to love you even though I know who and what you are and what I'm dealing with," I told him one night, towards the end of our relationship, before shutting my bedroom door behind me.

He had nothing to say to that. He made no attempt to fight for this relationship...to fight for *us*. I just couldn't handle who he was anymore. Like being with Dr. Jekyll and Mr. Hyde, since his moods were unpredictable; and to a terrifying degree. That's when I realized at that very moment this wasn't going to work.

I really thought I could change him by helping him see that there was genuine love in me and that I could show him what true love was. That maybe he never was given the chance to feel something like this. And that maybe what I had to offer would transform him.

It was Monday morning and I was tired because I didn't get much sleep the night before. I was also wearied from the stress he was putting me through.

I was so drained from everything. Everything that I had gone through just to make him happy. Because I wanted something that was a lost cause long before I knew it was. I felt so fatigued as my mental and emotional exhaustion sapped all my physical energy. Then, out of the blue, I collapsed at work.

I awoke to find myself surrounded by paramedics, but I refused to be taken to the hospital in fear that I would have to be transferred to a psych ward for tests I just wasn't in the mood for. I regained my composure as quickly as possible and powered through the rest of the day.

I arrived home around 4:00 pm and he was still asleep on the couch having been up all night playing that stupid online game.

I reminded him that the electric company was going to transfer the balance of my bill from the old place to our new one. I asked him if he was okay with helping to pay it and he said he was. I didn't remember what the amount was and when I reached for the bill, which I thought was in my backpack, it wasn't there. It was at work.

I came home the very next day during my lunch break to collect his half so I could pay it.

He then told me, "I'm not helping you pay that bill!"

Of course, I thought!

"You told me that you would help," I reminded him.

"I never said that! And why the hell would I help you with a bill that I had no part of?" His face turned beet red in the midst of his obstinate refusal.

"You said you'd help pay it! You told me yesterday you would! Why are you doing this?"

"F____ you! I'm not paying nothing m____ f____! I'm leaving out of here in three days anyway! You are a crazy, toxic woman and I can't stand being with you!"

I was taken aback and shocked to immobility. I was at a complete loss for words.

"Truth is, I just want to be your friend now and that's all," he then proceeded to say.

Just like that. He would move on to the next.

Thing is, narcissists like him jump from woman to woman; using others in every way possible to get and do things for them they otherwise wouldn't for themselves. They lie incessantly to get what they want out of people, reeling them in at the beginning of their relationships, making promises of forever, constantly declaring their love, and showering them with gifts (love-bombing) to make it easier for their victims to fall into their trap. Then, when they have you where they want you, they criticize you, insult you, and make you feel inadequate and worthless. Because they're now dominating you. They make you co-sign for their houses, cars, or apartment leases, and then once they get all they want out of you, they're done and that's it. Without warning; without an explanation (or they make up a silly excuse); and more often than not, without closure. At least he was leaving, though, after what he said the night he insinuated he'd at some point physically harm me.

I was standing in front of the coffee table and I glanced over at his set of keys lying there. So, at that moment, I realized I have had it. I couldn't take this anymore. Suddenly, I snatched the keys in one quick grab and ran towards the door.

"GIVE ME MY DAMN KEYS BACK!" he screamed.

"NO! If you are not going to help me with the bills! If you are leaving anyway—why should you have them!? You won't be having these keys anymore," I yelled back. I regained control and put my foot down.

Seeing his expression. Seeing how furious he quickly grew; like a ravenous mountain lion, he was out for blood. I knew that Satan had taken over him completely.

"GIVE ME MY KEYS RIGHT NOW OR YOU'RE GOING TO SEE A SIDE OF ME YOU'D WISH YOU'D NEVER SEEN!" screamed the devil.

"NO!" I shouted.

I had his keys and my phone in one hand. As I ran and opened the door, he came charging at me, cussing and screaming at the top of his lungs.

When the door was ajar, I reached in between with my left arm. He threw his weight on the door with so much force that it basically felt like my arm was crushed, which caused me to lose my grip on both the phone and keys, which fell to the ground outside the door.

I was completely bent over, screaming in agony. It felt like my arm was broken. I was sobbing from the intense pain. I pushed open the door and grabbed the phone and keys with the other hand and ran. But then, I realized I didn't have my car keys, which meant I had to go back inside and get them.

I pushed Shamari hard out of the way and ran in and quickly grabbed my car keys.

"Give me my keys!" he yelled as he came after me.

"No! I said you're not getting them back!"

He then held the door closed with his foot and hand. He refused to let me leave.

"Just give me the keys and I'll let you go," he said more calmly.

I paused just for a moment, glanced briefly in the direction of the patio door and then rushed towards it. He came after me, outpacing me and then held closed that door tightly as well.

Then, it was back to the front door! Then back to the patio door! Then the front door and then back and forth and back and forth several more times!

"I'm calling the police!" I finally told him.

"Go ahead! Do it! Do what you got to do! I don't care anymore!" he shouted.

"Yes! I'm calling the police when I get back to work and by the time I get back home you better be gone!"

He then let go of the front door and I exited quickly, hoping that that was the last time I'd ever have him near me again.

I returned to work, which was only an 8 to 10-minute drive. By the time I got there my arm was beginning to swell pretty badly. I was in agonizing pain as well, which alarmed my coworkers and everybody at the office. They asked what had happened and I told them. They pressed it upon me to call 9-1-1, which I did, and explained to the operator that I was terrorized by my boyfriend and that he closed the door on my arm. EMTs and police arrived several minutes later and I was then transported to the hospital.

By the time I arrived, my arm had swollen even more and I developed severe bruising. My blood pressure was also dangerously high due to the trauma of the event.

The police took my statement and took a careful look at my arm as they wrote down a description of the injury. They also wanted to see how severe the injury was to see if it warranted Shamari's arrest. They assured me it did and I was relieved to know they were going to take him in shortly thereafter.

The doctor returned with results from the x-ray and ensured my arm had no breaks or fractures, but that the swelling and bruising would take some time to heal.

It was only about a half-an-hour later that Shamari was taken into police custody. I was granted an emergency protective order so he couldn't try to contact me or return to the apartment.

He only spent a day in jail before I got a call at work that he was released.

I had to return to court in the next few days to get the protective order extended. Shamari didn't have the guts to try and return to the apartment, thank God. I had no idea where he was and I didn't care as long as he wasn't anywhere near me anymore.

Several days later, I appeared in court and the judge ordered the protective order to be extended an entire year, which Shamari was unable to appeal.

I felt a great sense of relief and felt safe, finally. This chapter was done. It had come to a close. And Satan was no longer in my life. This monster I was able to defeat and I was no longer bound to him. It was time to recuperate. To shift my focus and rebuild. To admit my faults but come away with this with my head held high. And…it was time I apologized to God for being so naïve, petty, and negligent. It was time to ask God for His forgiveness.

15

I had to return to the hospital the next day because of total numbness in my fingers. I wanted to make one-hundred percent certain nothing was in fact broken or fractured. The doctor informed me that the swelling in my arm was pressing a nerve, which was causing the numbness and the overall loss of feeling in my fingers, but that it wasn't anything serious.

A part of me did miss him, but a much bigger part knew I would've been in a dead-end situation had I stayed in the relationship. Honestly, I don't think he himself had any intention of staying in the relationship as he made that abundantly clear in the end. But it was all over and that was the best thing that could've happened to me.

I knew I'd see him at least twice more because we had to make our appearances in court and at some point, he did have to come and get his belongings. But I told him he couldn't return to the apartment without a police officer present. That was the only way I'd let him back into my home.

He eventually returned to get his possessions and an officer was there to make sure nothing happened. I met him outside at the parking lot and he did look sorry for what he did. But I wouldn't regress. Not anymore. You got violent with me, Shamari, I thought. And I'm not one of those women that will let her boyfriend beat her up and then forgive him and take him back whenever he gives me sad eyes or gifts to make up for it.

"I really am sorry for what I did," he said. "I didn't mean to hurt you."

I then replied in the chilliest way possible, "But you did."

I got the locks changed just in case. Him secretly making multiple copies of the old key I did not put past him.

I hate to admit that I do miss him from time to time. It was hard getting used to not seeing him in the living room or lying on the sofa. It's bizarre the kind of stronghold narcissists can have on you. And anyone that's been in a narcissistic relationship would certainly understand; and that sometimes it's almost impossible to break free like it was for me.

Even when he was long gone, I left everything the way he arranged it. The furniture, his towels, the appliances, everything.

There were nights I'd cry almost nonstop over him. I loved him so much and still couldn't even tell you why; I just did. But I knew there was no way I could take him back. He hurt me once and I was certain he'd hurt me again and much worse next time. When you don't give a narcissist what he wants, anything goes. They can be killers too.

During the grieving stages of our recently-defunct relationship, I'd drive around and past all the places we'd go to together.

I told my therapist how I felt about this monster. I told her that the Holy Spirit would penetrate deep in my heart and warn me constantly this man was Satan and that he was going to destroy me. The Spirit kept telling me to get my bible out of the trunk of my car, read the scripture, and listen to His message, but I refused.

She then said in a manner that was very professional but also hinted warmness and sympathy, "You completely shunned God and opened yourself to letting evil take complete control of you. You let this monster in your house to satisfy his urges and your own. You willingly entertained him the way he wanted and you mistook lust for love, convincing yourself that what you were doing with him was okay because what you had with him had to be genuine. But Nikki, he abused you. He hurt you. And I'm sorry honey, but this man didn't love you. He never did. You made uncharacteristic choices that a strong Christian woman such as yourself never would've made had you seen through him from the start and not let yourself become so brainwashed and consumed by his manipulativeness. We all have needs, I'm totally understanding of that. We are all human. But we also have to draw a line somewhere and be more aware. We have to open our eyes and hearts and be mindful of narcissistic people's motives. Thing is Nikki…Satan is still winning if you are still hung up on him because even after he's long gone, what you're feeling now is exactly what he wants. If this man can't be in your life physically, he'll find ways to be in your life emotionally. Through memories. Reminders. Through gifts or items of clothing he may have left behind. But…open the trunk of your car and keep your bible close and never let it go. Pray to God and pray those demons out of your house and open your house back up to the Lord. Because in the end, all you got is you…and God."

Later that day, I did what she told me to do. I prayed hard for God and His angels to chase those demons and any reminders of him away. At first it was too difficult. I was still crying over him. But then I asked God to speed up the healing and recovery process. I had to remind myself he was no good for me and keep reminding myself of all the terrible things he'd done and said to me. That he was poison. I told Him I'm trying to let go, but it was so hard and I really needed His help.

In my next therapy session, I told my therapist that I've been praying desperately for God to speed up the process. But also, that I have not been able to move his washcloth from the place where he left it. That I was still sleeping in the t-shirt he wore. That I kept seeing him even when he wasn't there.

"Nikki, so you said you're asking God to help you move on more quickly, right?" she asked.

"Yes."

"But yet, you're still sleeping in the t-shirt he wore, correct?"

"Yes," I replied hesitantly, hanging my head in shame, knowing very well what she'd say next.

"Nikki, you're still sleeping with the devil. Remember I told you last session he was still going to try to find ways to be in your life even if he couldn't physically be there? Sleeping in his shirt is not moving on. When you wear that shirt, you got him wrapped around you. When you see that washcloth by the sink, there he is reminding you he's still there. Nikki, you've *got* to throw his shirt and washcloth and whatever else of his, in the trash. And you got to do it now!"

There was a long pause as I thought over what she said. She was right. Any reminders of him had to be ended for good. I had to wipe it all away.

"Wow! You are right," I said. "I definitely will throw them away once I get home. I promise."

As long as his belongings were there, *he* was there, I thought. I've got to let him go now.

After I returned home following the session, I immediately did what she told me to do. I threw away his shirt and washcloth and trashed anything and everything that was his or reminded me of him.

Three weeks later, I then began deleting the videos he sent as well as the pictures. I felt God encouraging me to do this because this was the only way Shamari would be nothing more than a distant memory. A mere blip; a small stain that would eventually come off

104

with each wash. I truly wanted God to help me get rid of any and all feelings I had for him.

I abandoned God when I decided to give my heart and my life to that monster. I was so far gone that, as I mentioned, I lost everything that defined who I was. I was unrecognizable to my family, my friends, and myself.

I'd come home in tears and feeling so overwhelmed. I felt so much had gone wrong and I knew it was because of my disobedience towards God. But I'm glad God didn't give up on me and rather got my attention by having this demon hurt me physically for the point to get across. And that I wasn't so quick and so willing to run back to him even after he hurt me.

After erasing all memories of him, I turned my attention back towards faith entirely. I started spending time reading His Word and praying and did this every day like I was finding my way back home. And my feeling towards that monster started slowly diminishing as I continued to ask God for strength and for independence. I was going to persevere—for my family, for my friends, for my faith, and for me.

I was now becoming the woman I wanted to be again and I was being made whole. I'm saying once I did this, God opened up the gates of heaven, welcomed me with open arms, and showered me with so many blessings I felt deep down I didn't deserve, especially since I hurt Him just like Shamari hurt me. The only difference is, though, I'm human and God knows that I'm only human. I get weak. I make mistakes. I screw up badly. But while my faith is shaken, it cannot be destroyed, because God knows there is hope for me. And where there's hope, there is purpose. I couldn't save Shamari because he didn't want to be saved. I wanted to be and that's why I'm here right now. I'm glad I ridded those evil forces from my home and allowed God's spirit to dwell in my space.

Once I was obedient, I found redemption. I found peace. I found life. So many great things happened and continue happening after I let God back in and as I found my security in Him. With Him, I found true love. And I fall more in love with Him every day and that love only continues to grow stronger and stronger because He is truly the One for me.

I rediscovered my passions. My strengths. And found the courage to break from the woman the devil tried to mold me into. Not only was my spirit unbroken, but so was my dignity and my faith in myself as well. And I think it is no exaggeration when I say God very much saved my life.

My advice is to always educate yourself on narcissistic relationships, especially if you feel you currently are in one, or got out of one that left long-term damage.

I have spoken with many who have been in my situation and feel as equally trapped and unable to escape.

I shared my story with a young lady in that kind of relationship in which she felt there was no way out. But I told her that that's the kind of power these people like to have over her and gave her some strong advice, which I hope she took.

I thank God always for reaching deep inside and showing me how wrong I was. As I penned all this to paper, I said to myself, "Girl! You were straight off-the-chain, big time disobedient! What were you thinking sleeping with a man that didn't want to be your husband and that didn't love you!"

I repented and repented and asked God for His forgiveness, grace, and mercy. I'm glad to be back on track and loving me for me again. I'm imperfect, but God knows how hard I'm now willing to try; and I will certainly put forth that effort for Him like He has for me.

My prayers go out to all the women (and men; since there is a man I personally know that recently cut ties with his narcissistic partner) who've fallen hard the way I did. To the women who've been manipulated by narcissistic people; who've been beaten by them; and who've been murdered by them.

The narcissist is charismatic and knows how to effectively win over the gullible. The narcissist convinces you that you are something you're not; only because they want to fashion you to be the definition of perfection in *their* eyes, without letting you be and embrace who *you* are.

They'll tell you you're powerless—useless. They'll make themselves out to be the victims in any and every situation and persuade others to even believe they had every right to hurt you, to cut you down, and make you feel worthless because they were simply preserving their pride and dignity that doesn't truly exist.

They tell you they love you, want to marry you, and have kids with you because they know that's exactly what you want to hear. They systematically fashion their relationships in a way that would allow them to gain complete control, because control is something the narcissist will never relinquish, especially control of others, even if it kills them or the other person.

Never convince yourself that fake love is better than no love. That you'd rather be with an abuser than be alone for the rest of your life. Your choices are yours regardless of so-called societal norms and outdated ideas that if you're childless, unmarried, or single, that you're lost—and a loser.

And always remember, it's better to be happy alone than to be miserable with someone else, especially if that person is toxic and trying to rip your faith; your self-worth, and your identity from right under you.

Shamari was to appear in court September 13, 2021 for charges of domestic violence. He was facing up to one year in prison and a $2,500 fine.

He ended up being a no-show and is suspected to have fled the Commonwealth of Virginia.

The judge signed an interstate extradition order that would demand other states to deliver Shamari back to the Commonwealth of Virginia to face sentencing. There are also warrants out for his arrest in two other states.

Nikki J. Moore has not heard from Shamari or had any contact with him since he collected his belongings.

The Narcissist and Me

The Relationship That Should Not Have Been

<u>The Signs</u>

1. Narcissists have low self-esteem
2. They have the tendency to be very charming and charismatic.
3. They monopolize the conversation, usually talking mostly about themselves and touting their achievements (whether they are real, fictitious, or exaggerated).
4. Narcissists like to look great.
5. They feed off of people's compliments.
6. They are apathetic and typically lack feelings of sympathy, empathy, and compassion.

7. They gaslight people (manipulation and emotional and psychological abuse).
8. They will put others on a pedestal before becoming critical/hypercritical of them.
9. They have difficulties accepting any kind of criticism.
10. They have to always be right.
11. They are mostly unapologetic.
12. They like to change facts and details.
13. They are demanding, especially when demanding the "best!"
14. They have to always win.

Afterword

September 13th came and I had to appear in court at 9:00 am. My stomach was in knots and nervous just wasn't a strong enough word to describe how I was feeling that day and what I was going through mentally and emotionally.

I knew he would be ready to act, memorizing a script filled with lies that would make me the villain and discredit me in every way possible. He would've manipulated the judge too and deliver his lines in the most charming and charismatic way he knew how.

Thankfully and blessedly, I had strong support with me. She was one of my best friends and she was also a survivor of domestic violence. So, it was comforting having her there with me, to hold my hand and guide me through this.

But, during my agonizing wait for our case to be called, my ex-boyfriend was late. Finally, it was time for him to face the judge and he was still a no-show. He was admitting guilt, but refused to let himself be stripped of his so-called "pride," that he decided to cower and ditch his court appearance instead of verbally confessing his wrongdoings!

As this book closes in on publication, he is still wanted in several states.

Please ladies; be careful who you allow in your life. And men; be careful too. Remember, what looks good isn't always good. And if it seems too good to be true...it is.

Head up and God bless.

Thank you

First and foremost, I would like to thank my Lord and Savior Jesus Christ for bringing me out of that relationship and healing my self-inflicted wound.

My family for their continuous support.

Stephanie Davis & Kimberly Wheeler- My 2 best girlfriends who was there through all my drama!

Matthew J. Sam- For editing my book and for designing the covers.

Other works by Nikki J. Moore

How I Made It Through for Your Glory

(Available at Lulu, Barnes & Noble, Walmart, and Amazon)

The Journey Continues for Your Glory

(Available at Lulu, Barnes & Noble, and Amazon)

Shhh! Don't Tell

(Available at Lulu, Barnes & Noble, and Amazon)

Coming soon

How I Made It Through for Your Glory: The Play

Written and adapted for the stage by: Trae Skinner

Coming December 2021